Audio Access Included

BOSSA NOVA GUITAR

ESSENTIAL CHORD PROGRESSIONS, PATTERNS, RHYTHMS AND TECHNIQUES

PLAYBACK+

Speed • Pitch • Balance • Loop

To access audio visit:
www.halleonard.com/mylibrary

Enter Code
7091-8675-8770-9248

BY CARLOS ARANA

ISBN 978-1-4234-2519-9

HAL•LEONARD®
CORPORATION

7777 W. BLUEMOUND RD. P.O. BOX 13819 MILWAUKEE, WI 53213

In Australia Contact:
Hal Leonard Australia Pty. Ltd.
4 Lentara Court
Cheltenham, Victoria, 3192 Australia
Email: ausadmin@halleonard.com.au

Visit Hal Leonard Online at
www.halleonard.com

CONTENTS

Introduction 4

Chapter 1: BASIC CONCEPTS
Harmony 5
Rhythm 8

Chapter 2: STYLES THAT INFLUENCED BOSSA NOVA
Samba 9
Samba Cançao 13
Jazz 14

Chapter 3: RHYTHM
Right Hand Technique 15
Graphic Representation of the Rhythmic Patterns 15
Adding the Bass 18
Anticipating Chord Changes 19
Bass Notes in Bossa Nova 22
Muting 22
Bossa Nova Rhythm Patterns 24

Chapter 4: HARMONY
Preliminary Concepts 30
Bossa Nova Chords 30
Bossa Nova Chord Progressions 33

Chapter 5: PRACTICAL EXAMPLES
Pattern 1 37
Pattern 2 39
Compound Pattern: 1 + 2 41
Pattern 3 44
Pattern 4 48
Pattern 5 52
Pattern 6 56
Pattern 7 57
Pattern 8 60
Miscellaneous Patterns 61

Chapter 6: COMPLETE SONGS
Song 1 64
Song 2 68

Guitar Notation Legend 72

INTRODUCTION

Bossa nova, an internationally popular style of Brazilian music, was originally developed in Rio de Janeiro, in the late fifties. Precise definition of its origins is uncertain given that there were a number of contributing factors and influences, many of which took place simultaneously and all of which can be considered legitimate precursors. Most musical historians agree, however, that the official "birth" of bossa nova occurred with the 1958 release of Elizeth Cardoso's *Canção de Amor Demais*, on which a young guitarist named João Gilberto played a song called "Chega de Saudade" written by Antonio Carlos Jobim and Vinicius de Moreas. The second defining moment, and the one that truly established the classic sound of bossa nova guitar, was the release of Gilberto's first album as a solo artist, also titled *Chega de Saudade*, later that same year. It was on this album that Gilberto beautifully demonstrated for the first time all of the principal rhythmic, harmonic, and melodic characteristics that have come to define bossa nova.

Gilberto's work on that record, as well as on his two subsequent albums, was musical genesis. It influenced not only the entire bossa nova movement but also subsequent generations of Brazilian pop musicians. It also established a strong connection with American jazz musicians, many who began to include elements of bossa nova in their own compositions and repertoires. This, in turn, led to a number of albums that had an unprecedented impact around the world. Many of these recordings are still popular today, including such classics as Antonio Carlos Jobim's *Garota de Ipanema* (Girl from Ipanema), the title track of which is arguably the most popular bossa nova song ever written.

Bossa Nova Guitar is intended for a wide range of guitarists, from those with little experience in complex musical styles like jazz, Samba, or Bolero to highly trained professional guitarists looking to expand their musical palettes. To meet the needs of such diverse groups, the first chapter provides a background in bossa nova—related theory so that the reader can better understand the basic concepts that will then be applied in the examples and exercises found in the later chapters.

Chapter 1

BASIC CONCEPTS

This brief review is intended as a refresher on the basic concepts necessary for understanding, assimilating, and playing the harmonies and rhythms that compose the bossa nova style.

HARMONY

Harmony is the study of the structure, progression, and relationships between the chords that serve as the tonal basis for any melody. In this book, harmony within an individual chord is called *vertical harmony*, and the manner in which chords are played one after another is referred to as *horizontal harmony*.

Our study of vertical harmony examines the way that notes are combined to form chords of increasing complexity. For example, C7♯9 is more complex than a C major triad, as it contains flatted 7th and sharp 9th degrees.

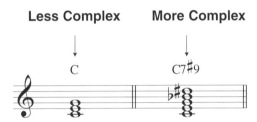

Horizontal harmony refers to the relationship between a series of chords in which some tonal criteria, such as voice-leading or counterpoint, is used to link them together. An example of horizontal harmony is tri-tonal resolution, where the "tension" produced by one chord is released by the one that follows it.

For example, in the C7–Fmaj7 progression below, the ♭7th (B♭) and 3rd (E) of the C7 chord resolve down a half step to the 3rd (A) and up a half step to the root (F), respectively, of the Fmaj7.

Harmonic Characteristics of Bossa Nova

VERTICAL HARMONY: Chord Extensions and Alterations

The basic harmonic structure of bossa nova is built on seventh chords, commonly including extensions and alterations, while largely eschewing major and minor triads. For example, when composing or playing a bossa nova song, the sound of C major is expressed using more vertically complex chords, such as Cmaj7, Cmaj9, or C$^6_9$.

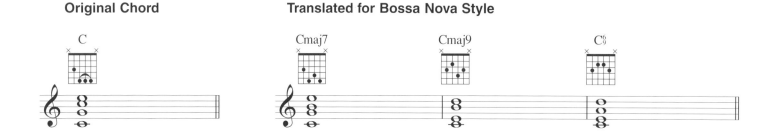

The same concept is used with chords that are already more complex than a major triad. For example, a C6, which is also a major chord, could also be substituted with C$^6_9$, Cmaj7, or Cmaj9.

Here are the possibilities for chord substitutions between chords that fulfill the same harmonic function:

- Maj7, maj9, and 6 chords can be freely substituted for each other.

- A m7 chord can always include a 9. Most m7 chords may also use an 11.

- Dominant 7th chords that resolve to major can be extended to a 9 and/or a 13.

- Dominant 7th chords that resolve to minor can include a ♭9, ♯9, and/or a ♭13 (♯5).

- Dominant 7th chords that do not resolve to another chord often can extend to a 9 and/or a 13.

- Diminished 7th chords generally can include any note that is one whole step (M2) above or one half step (m2) below any of its four notes.

HORIZONTAL HARMONY: Voice Leading

Chord voicings in bossa nova, particularly the bottom and top notes, usually move in sequential steps, often in chromatic fashion, to provide the crucial element of voice leading. Key to successfully using this approach is respecting the melody of the song while also creating a certain degree of melodic tension and tonal instability. The "overuse" of extensions (particularly 6ths and 9ths) as well as alterations (such as augmented and diminished 5ths and 9ths) is quite common in bossa nova, and it becomes particularly interesting when choosing voicings for accompaniment.

Lets look at a typical ii–V–I progression as heard in a jazz context. In the key of C it would be Dm7–G7–Cmaj7.

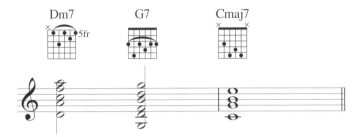

In the bossa nova style, however, these chords are modified in small but significant ways so that they become more harmonically complex, both vertically and horizontally. So the ii–V–I above, through the addition of extensions and a tritone substitution for the V chord, becomes Dm9–D♭9–Cmaj9, resulting in chromatically descending bass (D–D♭–C) and melody (E–E♭–D) lines that provide strong resolution to the C major key center.

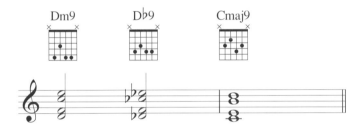

Here's another alternative, this time adding an altered 5th on the tritone substitution, and then substituting a bossa-friendly 6 chord for the maj7.

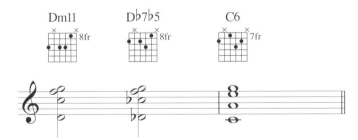

As you play through all three versions of that ii–V–I, pay close attention to the movement of notes (voices) within the chords as well as in the bass, and listen carefully to how each version differs from the others. You should recognize how, with voice leading, the horizontal transition between chords becomes more fluid.

RHYTHM

While a solid grasp of bossa nova harmony is necessary for learning the style, equally important is the element of rhythm. To begin, let's go through some basic definitions.

Beat: This is the basic unit of time. It is almost always what we instinctively tap with our foot when listening to, or playing, a song.

Tempo: This is the speed at which successive beats occur. It is indicated either in beats per minute (BPM), or with informal labels such as slow, medium, or fast.

Accent: This indicates that emphasis should placed on a specific note, usually at the beginning of a beat. Thus, we have beats that are "stronger" (played loudly) and beats that are "weaker" (played more softly).

Subdivision: This is the way in which the main beat is divided. If the beat is divided by two (or a multiple of two), it is referred to as being "simple"; if it is divided by three (or a multiple of three) it is called "compound."

Measure: The length of time that takes place between two strong beats, measured by the number of pulses that separate them.

Bass Line: This is the melodic line in the bass register. It supports the harmony and marks the rhythm.

Simplified Bass Line: As implied in the name, this is a simplified version of the bass line, often played by a percussion instrument.

The variations in the above rhythmic characteristics are what give bossa nova its unique feel, which we all know to be uniquely rhythmic. Keep this in mind as you move on to Chapter 2 and begin to play real bossa nova examples.

STYLES THAT INFLUENCED BOSSA NOVA

To really understand and play a musical style, it is important to know its roots and origins. In this chapter, we will look at the styles that influenced the development of bossa nova, both rhythmically and harmonically. This knowledge will serve as a reference point, and help you to understand how bossa nova has developed over the years.

Essentially, the rhythmic aspects of bossa nova were developed entirely by João Gilberto, as he masterfully fused together a variety of diverse influences, simplified them, adapted them, and in a certain way instilled them with a greater air of sophistication. But Gilberto had to start somewhere, and that's where we begin, with an overview of the basic stylistic elements of samba, samba Cançao, and American jazz.

SAMBA

Samba originated in Rio de Janeiro, where it is still popular today. It is rhythmically complex, with steady beats and syncopated rhythms simultaneously played by different instruments. For example, the bass drum often marks the offbeats, while the tambourine plays the syncopated backbeats and accents. It is from the blending of these two diverse elements that the basic sound of Samba is born.

This rhythmic complexity inspired João Gilberto's original right-hand technique. Known as his *batida*, it's a subtle and minimalistic simplification of the syncopated accents of the tambourine mixed with the steady beat of the surdo (Brazilian bass drum). His style of playing took the basic components of a Samba ensemble, in a conceptual sense, and then adapted them as his own, to create the bossa nova style.

Characteristics of Samba

The basic characteristics of a samba rhythm are:

- Medium to fast tempo
- Two beat measures (2/4 or 2/2 time signature)
- Sixteenth-note subdivision
- Syncopated accents, particularly in the fourth beat
- A simplified bass line that accents the second note of each measure

The Samba's rhythmic feel consists of a binary pulse accentuated every two beats, each one subdivided into four equal parts. This allows us to write Samba rhythms in the following two ways:

2/4: This is the time signature most commonly used in Brazil. The measure is composed of two quarter notes.

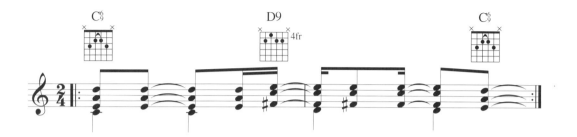

2/2: This time signature has two half-note beats, with four eighth notes per beat. This notation allows you to read in eighth notes instead of sixteenth notes.

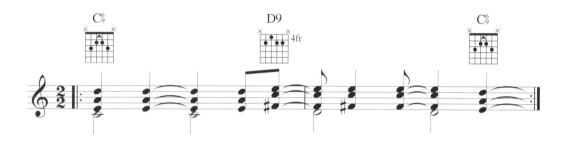

Origins of the Samba Rhythm

The rhythmic influences of samba came from traditional dance music, which were in turn influenced by other, earlier Latin-American styles. Here are the basic rhythms of some of those dances.

Habanera

And here are two variations on the Habanera rhythm.

Polca

And here are two of its variations.

Maxixé

Strongly influenced by habanera and polca, traditional Maxixé dance music was developed in Rio de Janeiro in the 1870s. Its basic rhythm pattern looks like this.

This rhythmic style is usually referred to as *Brasileirinho* (meaning: "a little Brazilian") and is the basis of samba. The most common variations of this rhythmic style are as follows.

Here are a few examples of other maxixé rhythms:

Originally, samba guitarists strummed the chords with a pick. Since electronic amplification had not yet been invented, using a pick was the only way to play a stringed instrument loud enough for a sizeable audience to hear. In the modern age of amplification and PA systems, however, samba and bossa nova guitarists have adopted the more versatile fingerstyle approach.

When playing bossa nova and samba fingerstyle, the thumb plays the bass notes, and the index (I), middle (M), and ring (A) fingers (referred to as the "IMA block" throughout the rest of this book) play the accents. It is important to keep in mind that, most of the time, the thumb will emulate the beat of the surdo (the percussion instrument in a samba ensemble with the lowest tone), and the IMA block will emulate the tambourine (the small drum that usually accents the syncopated notes in a samba).

Remember: The bass in samba accents the offbeat (just as the surdo would), meaning it plays the second beat of the 2/4 measure. This is extremely important to keep in mind when playing a samba, because it gives the samba its unique feel and makes it "move" as if it were a dance. This particular way of accenting the offbeat is directly related to the style's African roots.

Here is a typical samba rhythm:

Now let's take a look at a musical example typical of the "Samba Old School" (Velha Guardia). As you can see, the bass notes accent the offbeats while at the same time creating a secondary melody that often plays counterpoint to the main melody. This is also a commonly seen element of another style of Brazilian music called *Choro*, or *Chorinho*, which has also been referred to as "Brazil's Bebop" due to its complexity.

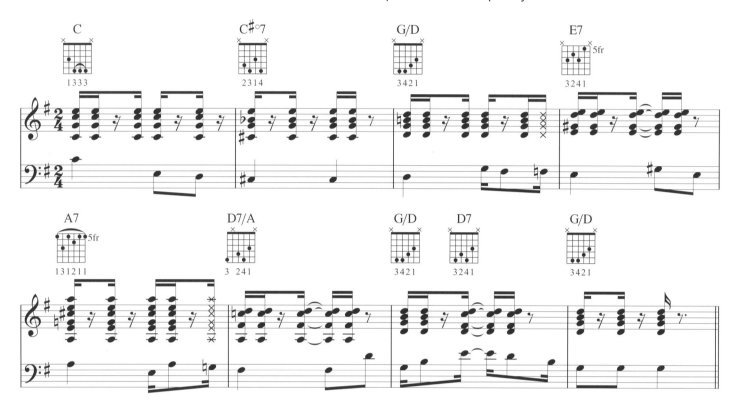

Here is an example of a more modern samba. The right hand uses a fingerpicking technique, and you can clearly see the simplified bass line.

SAMBA CANÇAO

Samba Cançao, also developed in Rio de Janeiro, shows clear influences from Central American music, particularly from the Bolero. As the samba Cançao was quite "in vogue" in Brazil throughout the fifties, its influence on bossa nova is clearly apparent.

Samba Cançao is played in 4/4 time, as opposed to samba and bossa nova, which are in 2/4. It's beyond the scope of this book to speculate why this convention is followed, but you should recognize that the bass note is played on the first and third beats (and occasionally on the fourth beat), with *equal intensity*.

Here is the basic pattern of a samba Cançao.

And here it is with a slight change in the bass rhythm.

Here is an example of a samba Cançao:

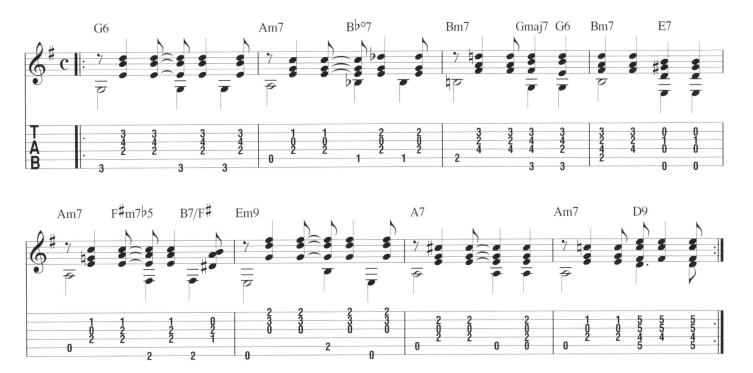

JAZZ

American jazz music was very popular in Brazil in the fifties. Harmonically, jazz favors altered and extended chords, and rhythmically, it often utilizes anticipated beats in its comping patterns. Both of these elements clearly influenced the first generation of bossa nova composers.

Here's an example of a typical jazz accompaniment pattern. Note how the use of altered chords and substitutions add both vertical and horizontal complexity, and lend themselves to effective voice leading.

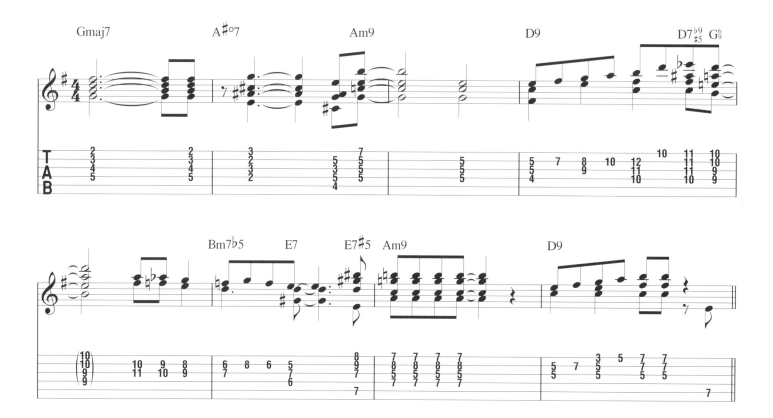

Chapter 3

RHYTHM

RIGHT HAND TECHNIQUE

João Gilberto's simplification of the basic samba patterns was quite controversial when he began playing them, and many other guitar players had difficulty adapting to this new style. Still, as time passed, Gilberto's approach became the new standard—not just for the guitar, but for all the other harmonic instruments as well.

Although he had simplified the patterns, Gilberto nonetheless played with a previously unheard of level of precision and subtlety, yet at the same time honored and maintained the original samba feel. João Gilberto's right-hand technique was borrowed directly from classical guitar technique. The thumb is positioned parallel to the strings, at the level of string set 6–5, whereas the IMA block is positioned perpendicular to the strings, over string set 4–1. Keep your thumb a good distance from the IMA block, to keep their movements as independent as possible.

As previously mentioned, the thumb is responsible for maintaining a steady beat, and thus the groove. Although the bass rhythms are both constant and symmetrical, it is important that they also be *balanced*, since this particular element provides the swing that is so vital to the bossa nova sound.

The IMA block, however, is used quite differently in bossa nova, and the technical complexity required merits a more detailed examination before we go any further.

GRAPHIC REPRESENTATION OF THE RHYTHMIC PATTERNS

In my teaching experience, I have repeatedly seen how difficult it can be for guitarists to learn rhythms with strong African influences, like samba or bossa nova. To simplify this task as much as possible, I have developed graphic representations of the rhythmic patterns used for one- and two-measure phrases. These representations help the guitarist "feel" the rhythms, which is fundamental to playing bossa nova fluidly and with swing. Please keep in mind that these representations are only visual references; they only help if you use them in conjunction with the actual music they represent, watching the references while listening to the accompanying audio tracks.

As you now know, bossa nova is based on a two-beat measure, with each measure then subdivided into four notes. In the graphic representation it looks like this:

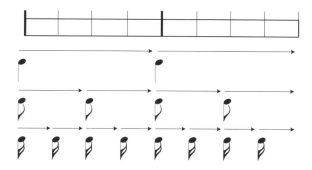

Each box represents one sixteenth-note subdivision, two represent an eighth note, and four represent a quarter note. Finally, all eight boxes together represent a complete measure of 2/4.

We'll use the following symbols to represent the attacks and note durations in each example.

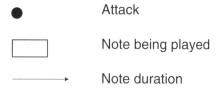

●   Attack

☐   Note being played

⟶   Note duration

African-based rhythms have always been closely linked to dance movements, and there are certain inherent difficulties in translating this to standard musical notation. These graphic representations clearly show both the attacks and note durations for each type of rhythm, and thus provide an effective tool for transmitting the feel of these various rhythms.

Before we get into the dance-based rhythms, here are several graphics depicting basic rhythmic values, to help you get comfortable with them. This first sample measure contains two quarter notes.

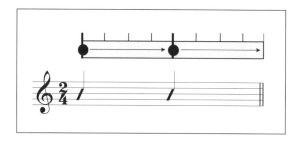

Eighth notes look like this in the graphic format:

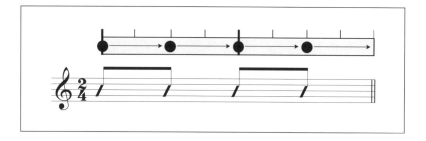

And sixteenth notes look like this:

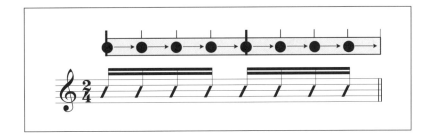

Now, let's look at a simple pattern, such as a typical reggae beat, where the second eighth note of each beat is played.

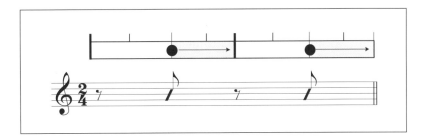

Here's a variation on the previous rhythm, where each eighth note is broken down into two sixteenth notes.

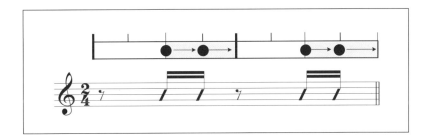

Now let's examine the more complicated rhythms of the Brasileirinho and the Maxixé.

Brasileirinho

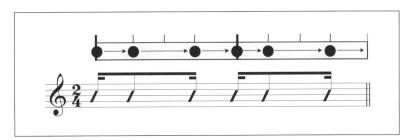

Maxixé

ADDING THE BASS

We will now add the bass notes, played by the thumb. In the standard notation, these are indicated with downstemmed notes, and the graphic representation of the bass notes appears below the standard notation staff.

Also, this section marks the beginning of the audio examples. Here, each new rhythm is presented first in graphic form, then in standard notation with tablature. For each example, first examine the graphic representation, to get a feel for that particular rhythm. Then play the example's accompanying audio track, following the graphic representation with your eyes as you listen with your ears. Next, play the audio track again, and use the standard notation and tablature to play along with it. Finally, play the example on your own, without the aid of the audio track.

 Tune Up

Track 1

In our first example, the IMA block plays an eighth-note rhythm, while your thumb plays a quarter-note rhythm

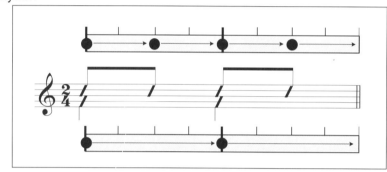

And here is an example using sixteenth notes for the IMA block, while maintaining a strong quarter-note pulse in the bass.

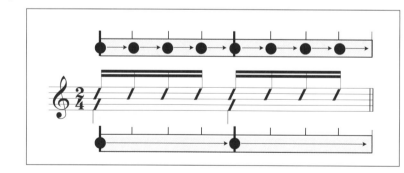

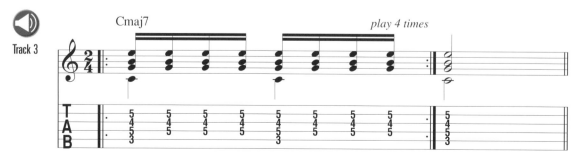

Now here's the Brasileirinho rhythm, as it sounds with a static Cmaj7 chord.

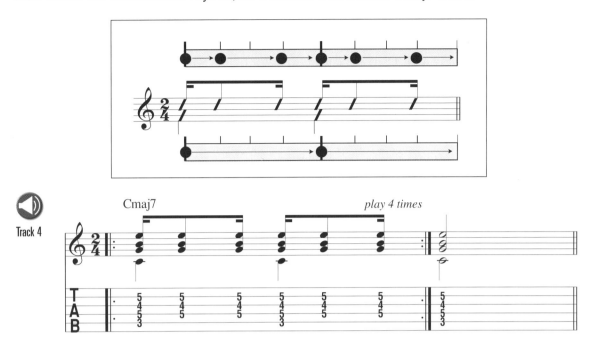

And now here's the Maxixé, also using a static Cmaj7 chord.

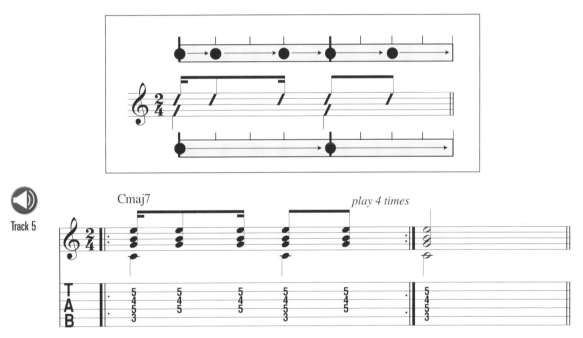

ANTICIPATING CHORDS CHANGES

When a note or chord is played on a weak beat, or in the weak part of a beat, we call it *anticipated*. If it is held over through a strong beat, we say it is *syncopated*. In Brazilian music the anticipated notes, with or without syncopation, are usually played as sixteenth notes.

Traditionally, harmonic instruments such as the guitar, piano, or cavaquinho did not use anticipation or syncopation in samba or other styles influential on bossa nova. These rhythmic practices were, however, quite common in American jazz accompaniment, and thus was a major influence on the playing of João Gilberto.

We will now look at examples of both approaches: playing on the "head" of the measure (without anticipating the beat), and then using syncopation.

For this first example, played without syncopation, we will use Gilberto's famous bossa nova groove the *batida* (which we'll call Pattern 1, for future reference).

In the next example, we add syncopation to the progression, using the second-most popular bossa nova rhythm (Pattern 2), which will get special attention when we look at strumming in chapter 5. Pay special attention to the way the arrows in the IMA block extend through the bar lines. Also, note that there is no end to the final arrow, as it would naturally lead into the next measure.

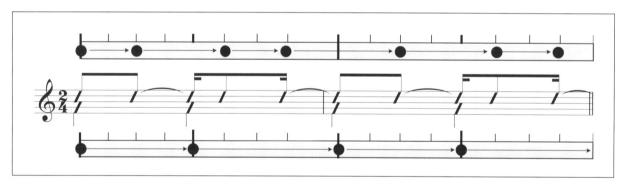

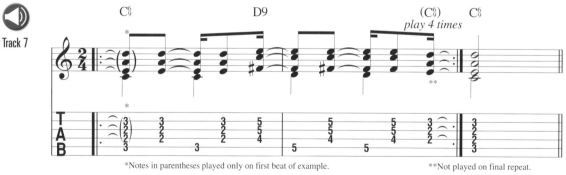

*Notes in parentheses played only on first beat of example.   **Not played on final repeat.

As you can hear, this syncopation adds an exciting "color" to the sound while making the progression more fluid, which is an essential element of bossa nova.

Next, let's take a look at a rhythm that features anticipation without syncopation, using bossa nova pattern 2.

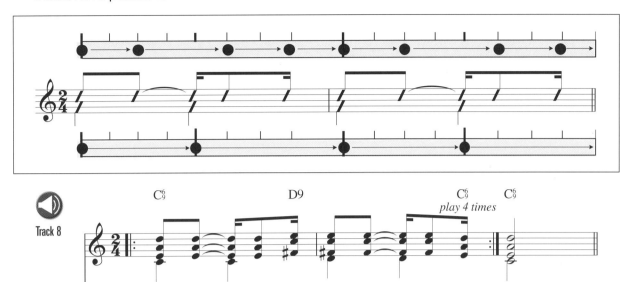

A chord progression containing two different chords in a single measure can include an anticipated chord change over the weak (second) beat. Although this anticipation will not be as noticeable as one played over the strong beat, the feel it creates is very similar, and worth considering here.

In this next example, we'll add a G7♭13 to the second measure of the C$^6_9$–D9 progression we just played, while also substituting the Brasileirinho rhythm, to create a weak beat syncopation in the second measure. Notice that the fourth measure does not contain the weak beat syncopation.

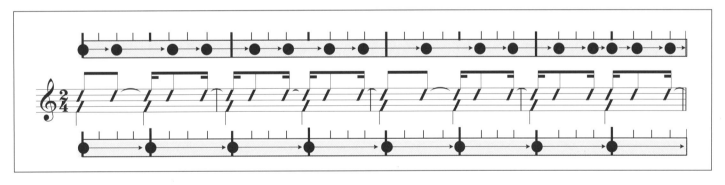

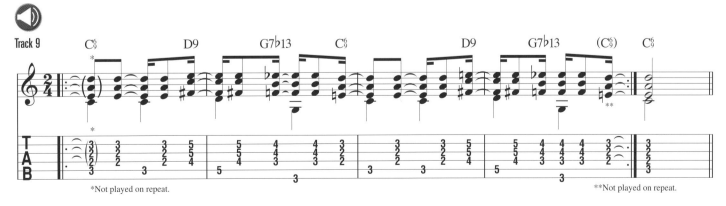

*Not played on repeat.   **Not played on repeat.

BASS NOTES IN BOSSA NOVA

Recall that when playing samba on the guitar, the bass notes simulate the role of the surdo, while in bossa nova it plays a similar role, but in a simplified manner. Here are some further refinements to this rule.

In bossa nova:

- **The offbeat is not accented.** Both beats of the 2/4 measure are played with the same emphasis.

- **It is NOT common to alternate the tonic with the dominant, or 5th.** In the original bossa nova style as played by João Gilberto, the tonic–5th alternation is not nearly as common as it is in traditional samba bass lines.

- **Bass notes are usually played on the sixth string.** Gilberto generally favored playing the bass notes on the sixth string, which gives added weight to the sound.

The following example demonstrates all three of these characteristics of the bossa nova bass line.

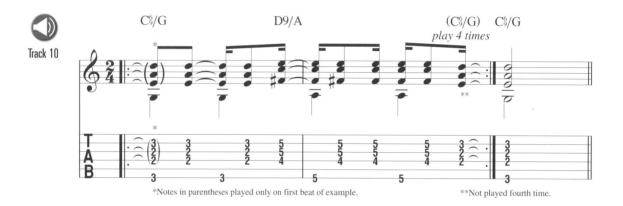

*Notes in parentheses played only on first beat of example. **Not played fourth time.

NOTE: Playing the bass notes on the sixth string sometimes means that the chord is being played in its second inversion (with its 5th in the bass). This can cause differences in the way the chords are identified. For instance, in the previous example, the first chord can also be called G⁶₉, and the second Am6. In these cases, let the song's key or mode be your guide.

MUTING

So far, every rhythm we've played has contained only ringing notes. But the use of rests, or subdivisions containing no notes, is a very common device in bossa nova rhythms. Rests are produced using a *muting* technique. This can be achieved in two ways: you can either slightly release your left hand's pressure on the strings, or you can touch the ringing strings with your right hand's fingers, to stop them from sounding. In bossa nova, the first approach is more common, and the one we'll concentrate on here.

In this first example we'll mute the final eighth note of the second beat.

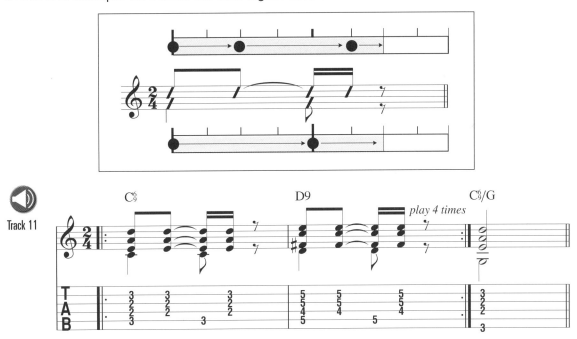

Track 11

Another way to notate this rhythm is to use the sixteenth–eighth–sixteenth rhythm pattern on beat 2 (as found in the Maxixé and Brasileirinho rhythms), placing a sixteenth-note rest on the final subdivision, and playing the preceding eighth-note subdivision in *staccato* fashion. When you stop a note from ringing for its entire duration, you're using the staccato technique. This is indicated with a small dot placed immediately above or below (depending on stem direction) the notehead. It sounds the same rhythm as using the two sixteenth notes, as above, but is more stylistically accurate for bossa nova.

Here's what it looks like in both graphic representation and standard notation. To hear what it sounds like, simply replay Track 11.

Muted notes are usually placed after eighth notes or dotted eighth notes that are not part of a syncopation. In the previous example, the eighth note that is tied to the sixteenth note is not muted because it extends into the following beat, but the dotted eighth note that follows is muted.

You must master left-hand muting to play bossa nova with the feel and fluidity for which it is known. Make sure you're comfortable with the technique before you move on to the next section.

BOSSA NOVA RHYTHM PATTERNS

In order to fully assimilate the bossa nova feel, you must become familiar with the various rhythm patterns used in the genre. In this section, we'll first examine eighteen rhythmic combinations of eighth and sixteenth notes, called *rhythm cells*, and then combine them to create popular bossa nova rhythm patterns.

Drilling these rhythms now will allow you to approach the practical examples in chapter 5 with confidence and in a relaxed state.

Eighth- and Sixteenth-Note Rhythm Cell Combinations

Each beat will be subdivided into four sixteenth notes. Each of these will be named as in the example below:

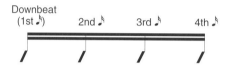

If the downbeat is preceded by a sixteenth-note syncopation, we have the following:

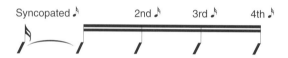

Here the beat is anticipated by a tied eighth-note:

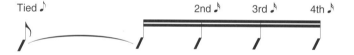

Now let's take a look at all of the combinations (including eighth- and sixteenth-note syncopations) upon which samba and bossa nova rhythm patterns are based. The following chart shows where the note is played in each sixteenth-note subdivision, with and without muting.

Cell	Tied ♪	Sync ♪	1st ♪	2nd ♪	3rd ♪	4th ♪	Rhythm Cell without Muting	Rhythm Cell with Muting
1	-	-	X	X	-	-		
2	-	-	X	-	X	-		
3	-	-	X	-	-	X		
4	-	-	X	X	X	-		
5	-	-	X	X	-	X		
6	-	-	X	-	X	X		
7	-	-	X	X	X	X		
8	-	X	-	X	-	-		
9	-	X	-	-	X			
10	-	X	-	-	-	X		
11	-	X	-	X	X	-		
12	-	X	-	X	-	X		
13	-	X	-	-	X	X		
14	-	X	-	X	X	X		
15	X	-	-	X	-	-		
16	X	-	-	-	X	-		
17	X	-	-	X	-	X		
18	X	-	-	X	X	X		

OK, now let's combine some of these cells to form a few of the rhythms that influenced samba.

Habanera: Rhythm Cell 5 + Rhythm Cell 2

Polca variation: (Rhythm Cell 6 + Rhythm Cell 2) + (Rhythm Cell 3 + Rhythm Cell 2)

As you can see, it is possible to create an almost unlimited number of combinations using these patterns. Try creating your own combinations, using chords you are familiar with. This exercise will help you learn how to play patterns based on sixteenth-note subdivisions and help you develop the ability to play this style in a relaxed, dynamic, and creative manner.

A large number of one-measure patterns can also be created using the patterns provided in the chart, including the two most important ones used in bossa nova: Pattern 1 and Pattern 2.

Pattern 1: Rhythm Cell 2 + Rhythm Cell 15

Pattern 2: (Rhythm Cell 2 + Rhythm Cell 17) + (Rhythm Cell 9 + Rhythm Cell 17)

Two-Measure Patterns

Bossa Nova often uses two-measure patterns, crafted from a virtually unlimited combination of rhythm cells. In this final section of the chapter, I'll show you several of the most commonly played bossa nova patterns, in their most basic form. Accompanying each example is its rhythm-cell makeup and its graphic representation. Note the use of staccato markings to indicate where chords should be muted. On the audio, I will first play the version without the muted notes, in measures 1 and 2, and then play the version with them, in measures 3 and 4.

Pattern 3: (Rhythm Cell 5 + Rhythm Cell 9 + Rhythm Cell 2 + Rhythm Cell 17) + (Rhythm Cell 12 + Rhythm Cell 9 + Rhythm Cell 2 + Rhythm Cell 17)

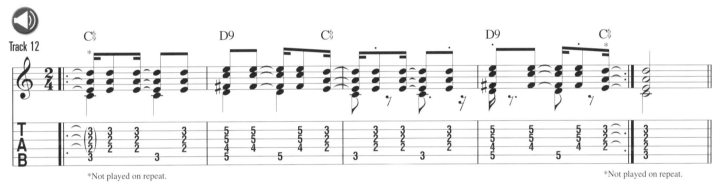

Track 12

*Not played on repeat.   *Not played on repeat.

Pattern 4: Rhythm Cell 2 + Rhythm Cell 5 + Rhythm Cell 12 + Rhythm Cell 8

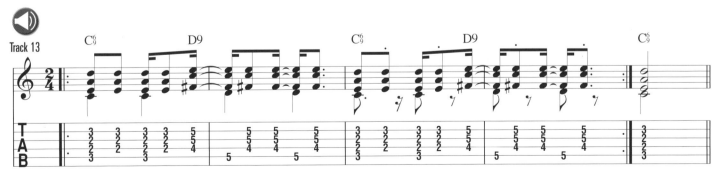

Track 13

Pattern 5: (Rhythm Cell 5 + Rhythm Cell 12 + Rhythm Cell 12 + Rhythm Cell 12) +
(Rhythm Cell 12 + Rhythm Cell 12 + Rhythm Cell 12 + Rhythm Cell 12)

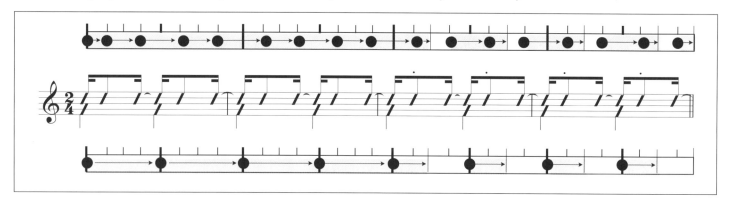

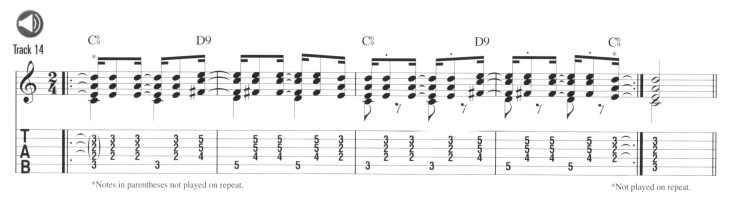

*Notes in parentheses not played on repeat.

*Not played on repeat.

Pattern 6: (Rhythm Cell 2 + Rhythm Cell 17) + (Rhythm Cell 12 + Rhythm Cell 9)

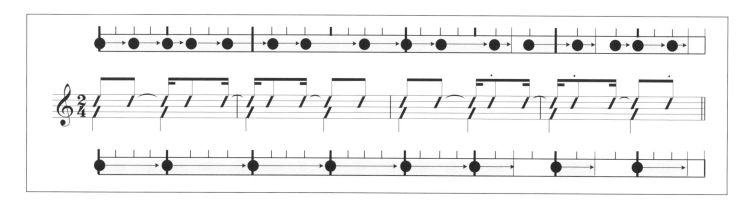

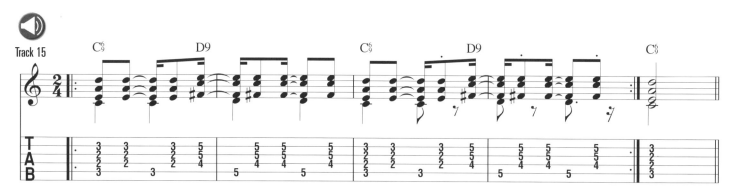

Pattern 7: (Rhythm Cell 3 + Rhythm Cell 8) + (Rhythm Cell 2 + Rhythm Cell 17) + (Rhythm Cell 10 + Rhythm Cell 8) + (Rhythm Cell 2 + Rhythm Cell 17)

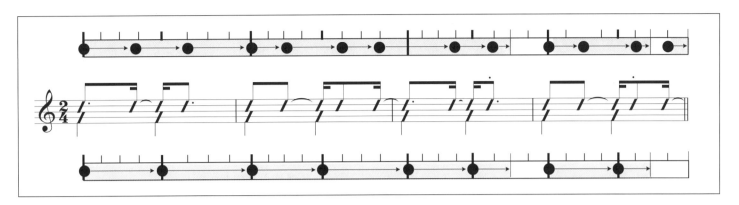

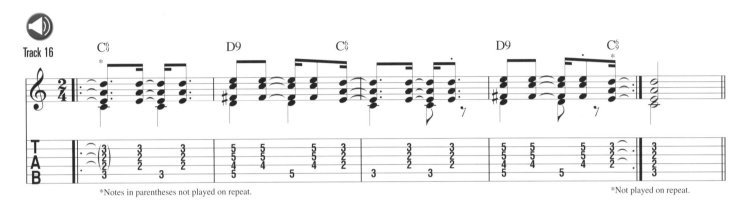

Track 16

*Notes in parentheses not played on repeat.

*Not played on repeat.

Pattern 8: (Rhythm Cell 3 + Rhythm Cell 10 + Rhythm Cell 10 + Rhythm Cell 10) + (Rhythm Cell 10 + Rhythm Cell 10 + Rhythm Cell 10 + Rhythm Cell 10)

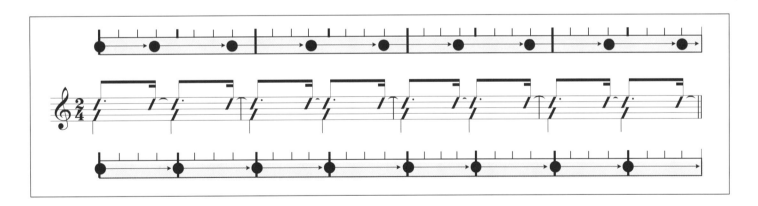

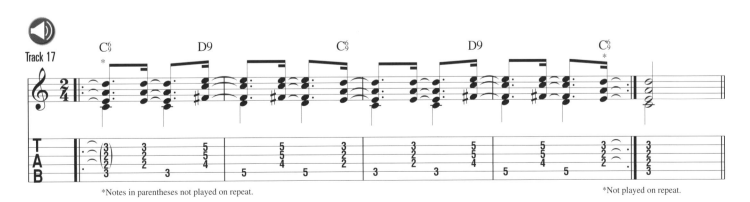

Track 17

*Notes in parentheses not played on repeat.

*Not played on repeat.

Chapter 4

HARMONY

PRELIMINARY CONCEPTS

João Gilberto was largely responsible for popularizing fingerstyle guitar in Brazil, when he applied the technique to the popular samba style. This new way of playing the guitar radically changed the focus of the instrument, because the percussive role that had been filled by playing with a pick was not possible using fingerstyle technique.

Like all Brazilian musicians of the period, Gilberto was strongly influenced by both samba Cançao and North American jazz. It was these two styles that largely contributed to the way he simplified the rhythm of samba while simultaneously creating more sophisticated harmonies. The beautiful result was a sound minimalist and modern, yet intimate.

One challenge Gilberto faced was that he could only play four notes with the thumb and IMA block, as opposed to the six notes that he could play using a pick. So, faced with the objective of maintaining the samba's essence while dealing with the limitations imposed by the right hand technique (combined with the need to play chords that are more harmonically more complex—both horizontally and vertically), Gilberto developed a new kind of harmonic vocabulary. The way he did this was to develop a large number of chords that would elevate the vertical harmony while facilitating the horizontal harmony's relationship with the rhythmic qualities that are in fact the basic essence of samba.

Memorize the chord catalog in this chapter and you will be able to comfortably navigate bossa nova compositions. It is extremely important to take the time to really learn all of these chord voicings and get them under your fingers, as the bossa nova rhythms are complex enough that you shouldn't have to also worry about chord shapes.

BOSSA NOVA CHORDS

I will begin by classifying the different types of four note chords (major, minor, dominant, and so on), and then within each type include extended and altered forms (e.g., maj9 and m7♭5). The chords are shown using standard five-fret chord frames. White dots indicate the location of the chord's root, so that you can move it to any key, and the black dots indicate the remaining notes of the chord. An "X" above the frame indicates that its string should not be played, whereas a "0" above the frame indicates an open string should be played.

Remember that chords containing an open string can be used only in the position indicated. These are considered to be "special cases."

maj7   **Major Chords**

maj9

Minor Chords

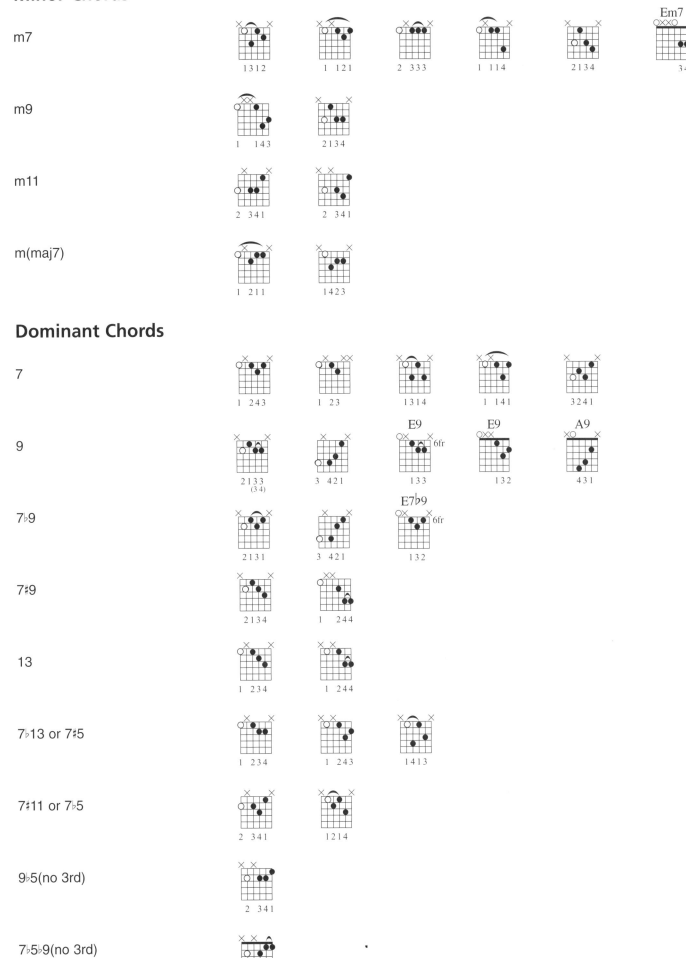

m7

m9

m11

m(maj7)

Dominant Chords

7

9

7♭9

7♯9

13

7♭13 or 7♯5

7♯11 or 7♭5

9♭5(no 3rd)

7♭5♭9(no 3rd)

7sus4

9sus4

9#11

7sus4♭9

6th Chords

6

$^6_9$

$^6_9$(no 3rd)

m6

m$^6_9$

Diminished Chords

°7

°7♭13

Half-Diminished Chords

m7♭5

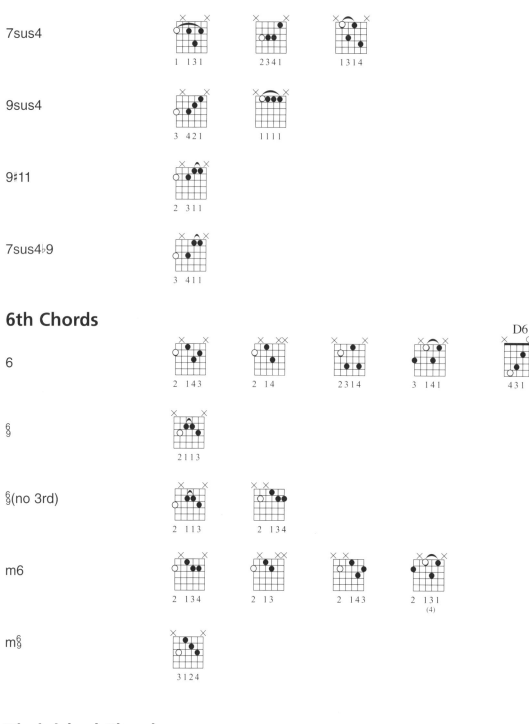
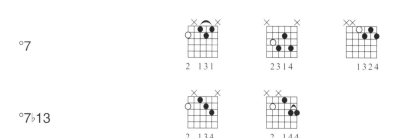
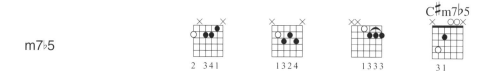

BOSSA NOVA CHORD PROGRESSIONS

Now that you've seen the chords, let's put them together into some bossa nova progressions. For now, don't worry much about the rhythms; instead focus on using the chord shapes from this catalog to play the progressions in time. For best results, play each rhythm slash as a quarter-note pluck, the first couple of times through, until you're comfortable forming the chord shapes and making the changes. Then, for more bossa nova authenticity, choose a rhythm pattern from the previous chapter and use that to play through these progressions. Next, choose a different rhythm pattern, and play through the progressions again, doing so as often as necessary to become thoroughly at ease with the changes. This will help prepare you for the practical examples in the next chapter.

Chord Progression 1

Chord Progression 2

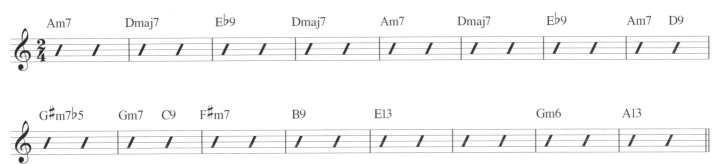

Chord Progression 3

Chord Progression 4

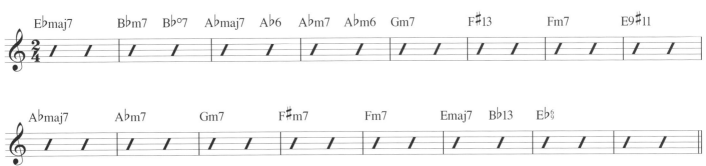

Chord Progression 5

Chord Progression 6

Chord Progression 7

Chord Progression 8

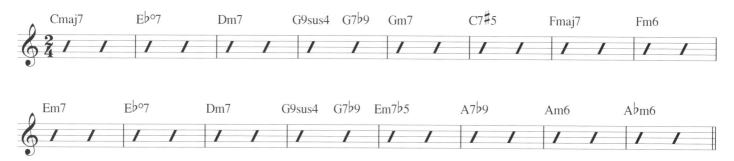

Chord Progression 9

Chord Progression 10

Chord Progression 11

Chord Progression 12

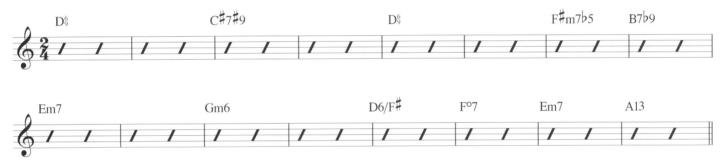

Chord Progression 13

Chord Progression 14

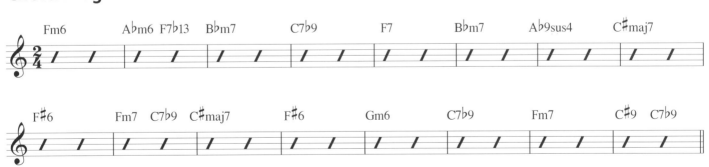

Chord Progression 15

Chord Progression 16

Chord Progression 17

Chord Progression 18

Chapter 5
PRACTICAL EXAMPLES

In this chapter, we will look at the rhythm patterns that are most common in bossa nova in combination with the chords and progressions from last chapter. These patterns were selected from several of the genre's most renowned artists, and in particular from the early work of João Gilberto. While it is possible to find other patterns in the bossa nova repertoire, most of them will be based upon the patterns presented here.

In order to create variations on the basic patterns, these examples include anticipated notes, syncopated notes, and tied notes. There are also variations created from the use of interpretive techniques, such as muting.

Each example also has a *Recommended Application*, to help you determine when and where (e.g., throughout a song, or only in the intro) it is best to use that particular pattern.

Finally, in developing the *batida* (groove), the patterns will be presented two at a time. The first patterns in this chapter repeat the same measure twice, whereas the rest are made up of two different measures.

PATTERN 1

This is the most common pattern in all of bossa nova. As simple as it seems, there is a great deal of underlying subtlety, and it requires patience and practice to play credibly. Pay close attention to the details, such as muting variations, to keep the phrase from becoming a monotonous rhythmic cliché.

The variations that include muted notes begin to give us an idea of the real significance of this pattern. The use of this interpretive technique makes this pattern much more useful in a variety of situations, including songs where it is the only pattern used throughout the composition. This is why it is so important to be able to play it perfectly at any given time.

Here is how this pattern looks with the inclusion of the muted left hand notes.

That rhythm can also be notated using a staccato mark, like this:

And here is another variation, with an even more pronounced staccato effect.

That can also be notated in this way:

The difference between the two is extremely subtle, and the first pattern is more commonly used in bossa nova.

Recommended Application: Use this pattern as the basic right hand batida throughout a composition, regardless of chord density or musical situation.

Track 18

This variation uses a more staccato feel on beat 2 of each measure.

Track 19

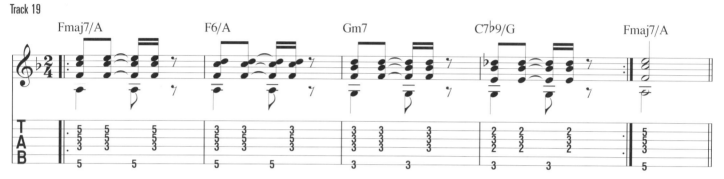

This following example alternates a non-muted and a muted variation through the first four measures and then employs heavy staccato-like muting in the final four measures.

Track 20

To help you clearly distinguish the muting variations from each other, try alternating between the variations every two measures, and then every other measure.

IMPORTANT: For simplicity's sake, all of the remaining patterns and variations will be notated in the basic way, *without* muted notes, though you may hear them played variously on the accompanying audio. Be sure to practice each pattern and practical example using all of the muted variations as well.

Variation 1

This variation on Pattern 1 adds an anticipated note before the syncopated sixteenth notes, making the pattern more rhythmically complex.

Recommended Application: As a variation of pattern 1.

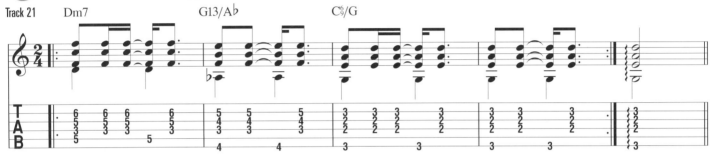

Variation 2

This variation, not often heard in bossa nova, is played without tied notes, adding an element of surprise to the feel, as demonstrated in measure 4 of the next practical example.

Recommended Application: As a sparse variation on pattern 1.

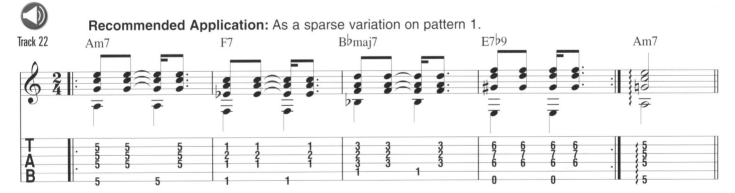

PATTERN 2

This is the second-most popular pattern used in bossa nova. The difference between this and Pattern 1 is the addition of a sixteenth-note syncopation over the downbeat of the first measure.

As with Pattern 1, Pattern 2 is rarely played in its most basic form (exactly the way that it is written here). It is usually only used when playing the same chord for two or more measures. For this reason we will immediately look at the version with muted notes.

Recommended Application: Use this pattern as the main batida, throughout the composition, regardless of the specific chord changes.

Track 23

*Notes in parentheses not played on repeat.

Variation 1

This variation introduces a new type of muting technique, in which you use left-hand muting, but your right hand still attacks the chord, to produce a muted "thud" on the last sixteenth note of the second beat. These "muted yet sounded" notes are called *ghost notes*. Using this interpretative technique is extremely important in achieving bossa nova's characteristic "swing."

In the example below, this variation is used in measures 2 and 4, to add a little spice to the rhythm.

Track 24

Recommended Application: Use as a variation on Pattern 1 or 2.

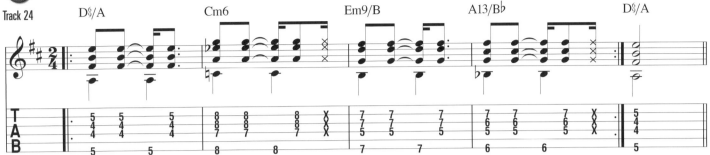

COMPOUND PATTERN: 1 + 2

This variation combines Pattern 1 (measure 1) and Pattern 2 (measure 2) into a compound bossa nova rhythm pattern.

Track 25

Recommended Application: Use this pattern as the main batida played throughout the composition.

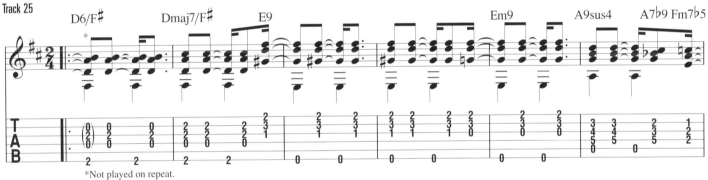

*Not played on repeat.

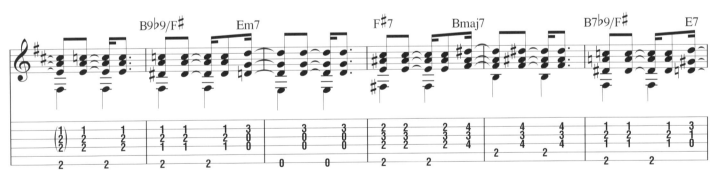

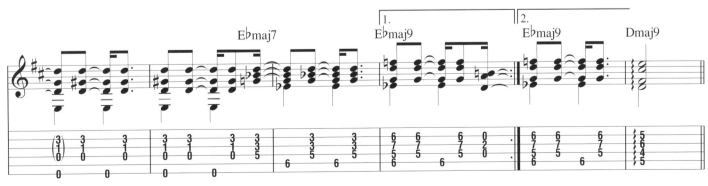

41

Here is the compound pattern made up of Patterns 1 and 2, played in reverse order (first 2, then 1).

This compound pattern has the same basic characteristics as the previous one, and is used the exact same way.

Track 26

Practical Example

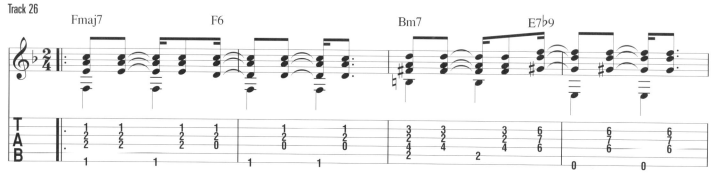

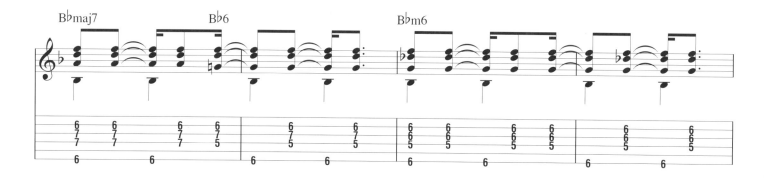

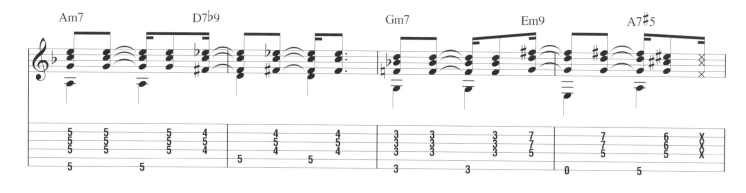

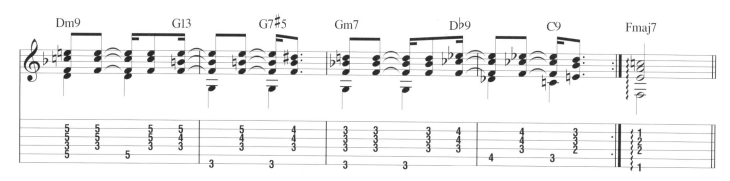

This example of the compound Pattern 1 and 2 represents the way Brazilian guitarists would play them.

PATTERN 3

This pattern is clearly derived from Samba, as demonstrated by the inclusion of the "Brasileirinho" style phrase in the first rhythm cell.

Recommended Application: This is used as the main "batida" for all different tempos (including samba, samba cançao, bolero, etc), particularly those with a strong samba-like feel (without losing its base in bossa nova). It can also be used as a variation of "batidas" based upon Pattern 2.

Practical Example

Track 28

Variation 1

In this variation, the syncopated note in the second beat of the first measure has been eliminated, thus giving the downbeat more emphasis.

Recommended Application: Used the same as Pattern 3. When used as an intro, however, straight eighth notes are substituted for the sixteenth–dotted-eighth rhythm on beat 1, as occurs in measure 1 below. The original pattern appears in the repeat.

Variation 2

This variation is a modification of the previous one, only here the second note of measure 2 is not syncopated, thus emphasizing the downbeat.

Recommended Application: Use as a variation on Pattern 3, or a substitute for Variation 1.

Track 30

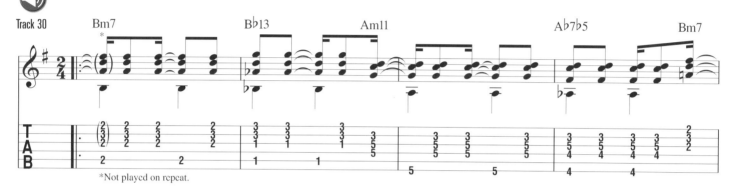

*Not played on repeat.

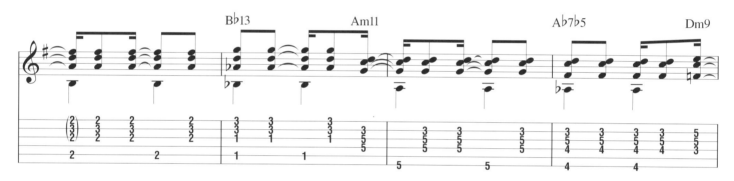

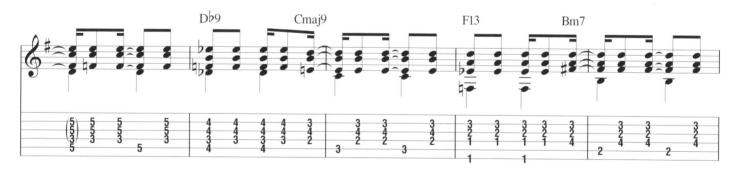

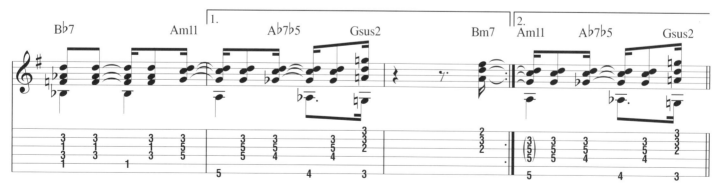

Variation 3

This one is similar to Variation 1, where the second beat of measure 1 is not syncopated.

Recommended Application: Use as a variation on Pattern 3, or a substitute for Variation 1.

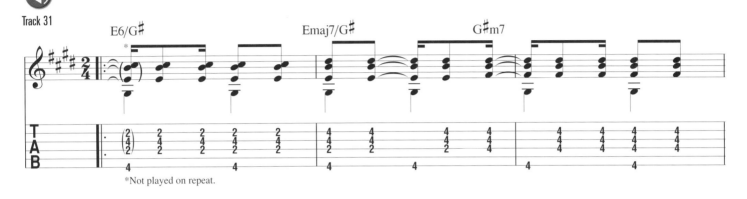

*Not played on repeat.

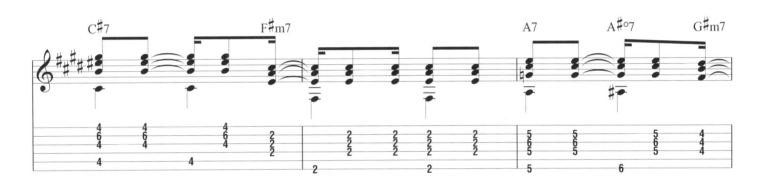

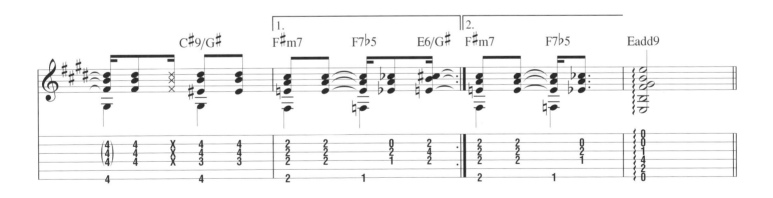

PATTERN 4

The defining characteristic of this widely used compound pattern is the large number of variations based upon it, all maintaining its original essence and sound. The songs that use this batida are almost always rooted in samba.

Recommended Application: Use as the main batida, played throughout the composition. It is usually played at medium to fast tempos (70–100 bpm).

Track 32

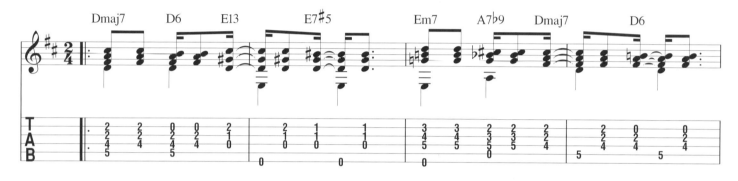

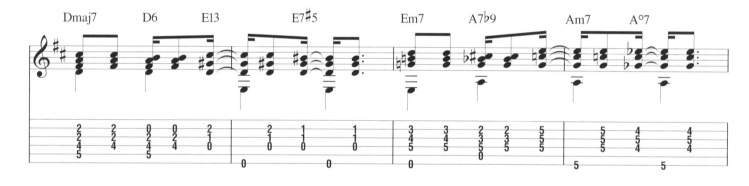

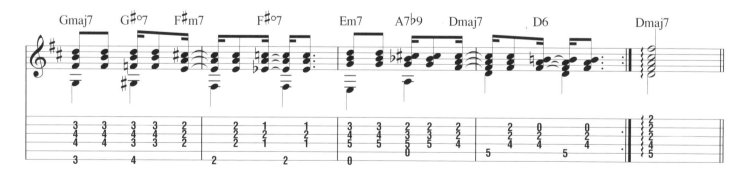

Variation 1

This variation on Pattern 4 simply eliminates the tie between measures 1 and 2.

Track 33

Recommended Application: Use the same as Pattern 4.

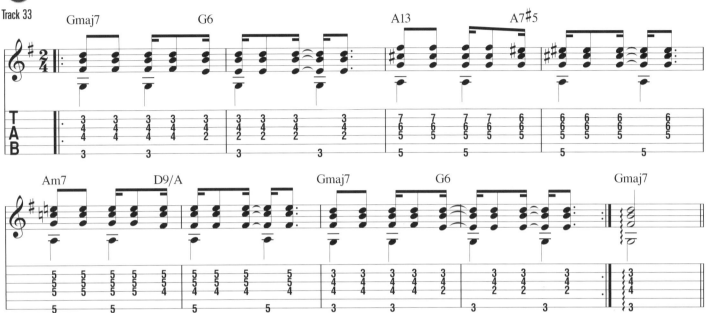

Variation 2

This is the most commonly used variation on Pattern 4.

Track 34

In this next example, you'll hear a strong staccato effect on the repeat (on the accompanying audio track), for even more variation.

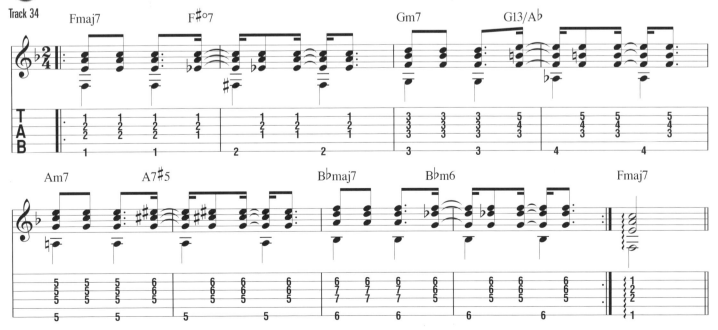

Other Variations

Variation 3

Variation 4

Variation 5

Variation 6

Variation 7

Variation 8

Variation 9

Variation 10

Variation 11

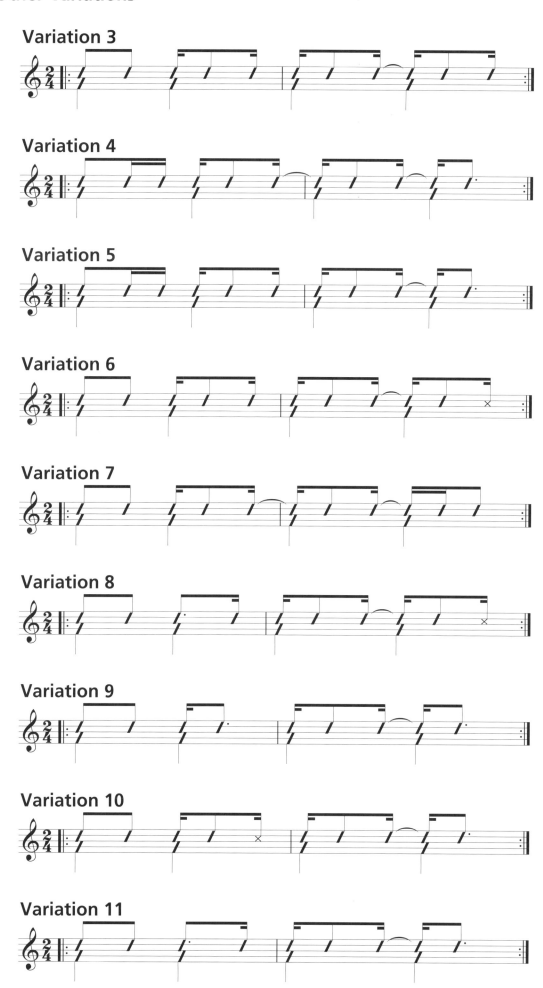

Recommended Application: Use as a variation of Pattern 4.

The next practical example cycles through Pattern 4 and its eleven variations, using a Gmaj7–G6–E♭maj7/G–E♭6/G progression throughout. The example is notated in rhythm slashes, with each rhythm pattern and variation clearly labeled. Here are the specific chord shapes used.

PATTERN 5

This is a prime example of a samba-based pattern, which is basically a repetition of the Brasileirinho rhythm cell with syncopation.

Recommended Application: It is usually used when two or more chords are played per measure, particularly in the final portion of a section, or in breaks left open for melody lines. It is sometimes used as a batida, especially in the early portions of a section, as the harmony behind a solo, or as accompaniment in conjunction with another harmonic instrument. It can be used with any type of composition and at any tempo.

Track 36

*Open low E string played first time through.

52

Variation 1

This variation is played without syncopation on the first beat of the pattern. The emphasis on the downbeat results in a stronger sound.

Recommended Application: Same as Pattern 5.

Track 37

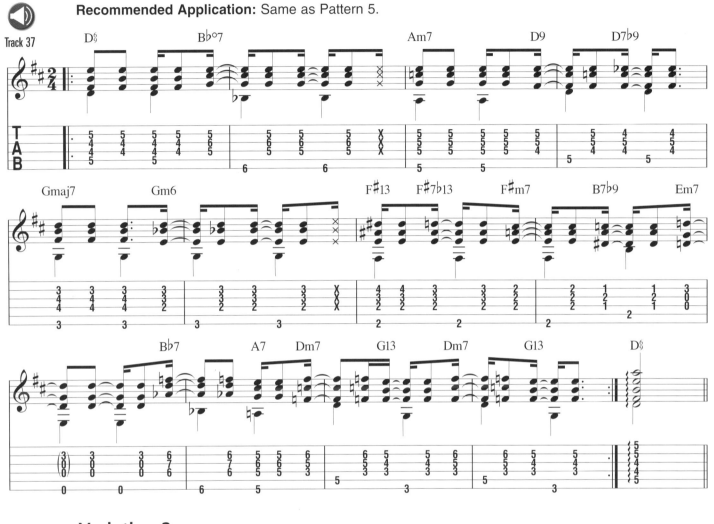

Variation 2

This variation emphasizes the downbeat attack not only on the first beat but on the second and third as well, clearly showing the characteristic sound of the Brasileirinho rhythm pattern.

Recommended Application: Same as Pattern 5

Track 38

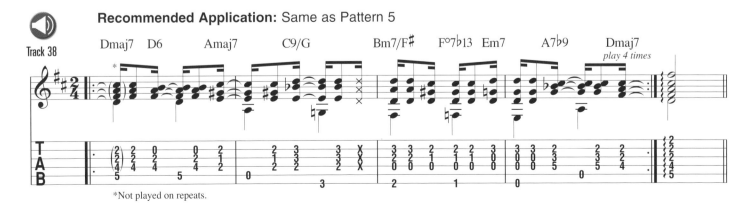

*Not played on repeats.

Other Variations

Variation 3

Variation 4

Variation 5

Variation 6

Variation 7

Variation 8

Variation 9

Recommended Application: Use as a variation on Pattern 5.

This next practical example contains Pattern 5 and all nine of its variations, demonstrated with a Fmaj7–A♭13/B♭♭–G13–G7♭13–Gm7–G°7 progression. The chord voicings used are shown in the frames below.

PATTERN 6

Recommended Application: This pattern is usually employed as a variation on batidas that includes some combination of Patterns 1, 2, or 4, and Variation 1 of Pattern 3. It also can be used as a batida, but this is rare in bossa nova.

Track 40

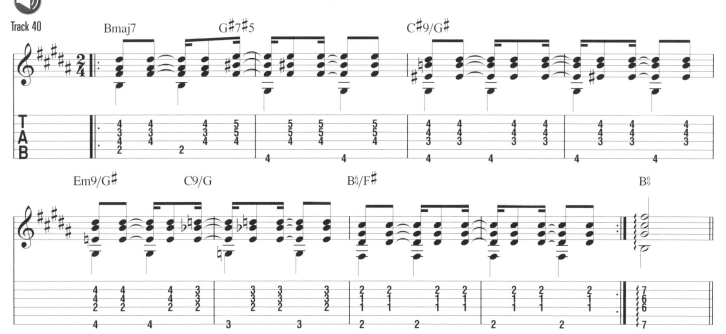

Variation 1

This variation is played without a tie to the first measure's second beat, emphasizing its Brasileirinho sound.

Track 41

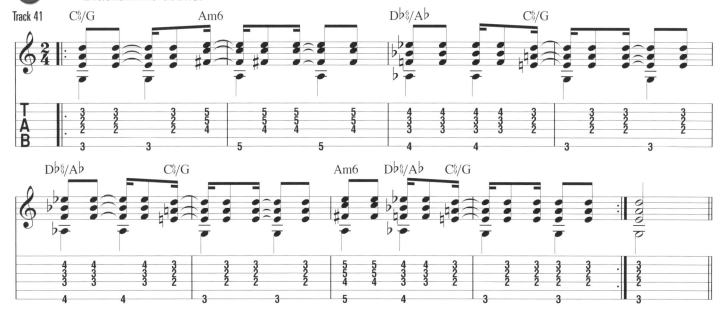

PATTERN 7

Recommended Application: Use as a batida. It can also be used as an element of surprise, adding dynamics and variety to the other patterns within a composition.

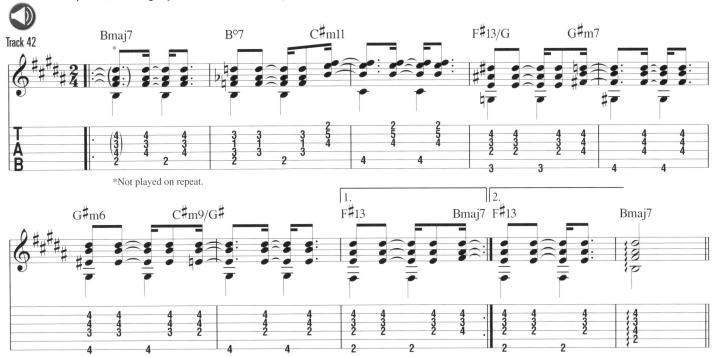

Variation 1

Recommended Application: Use the same as Pattern 7.

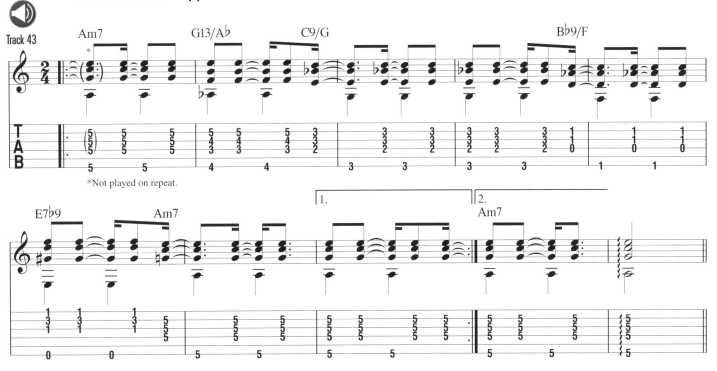

Variation 2

This variation uses a ghost note to anticipate the first beat of the second measure, thus decreasing emphasis on its downbeat.

Recommended Application: Use the same as Pattern 7

Track 44

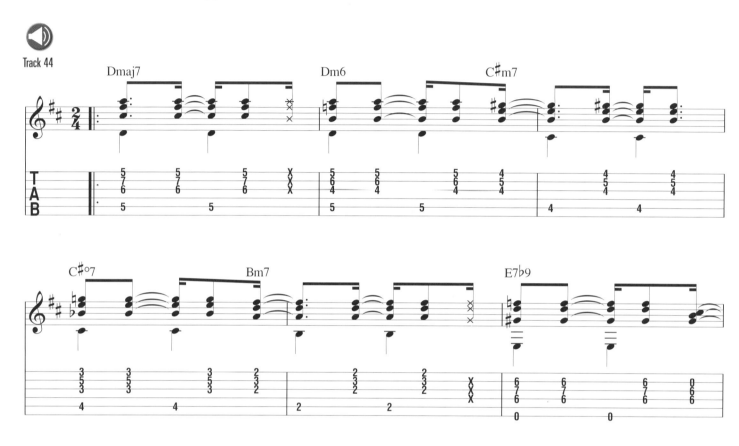

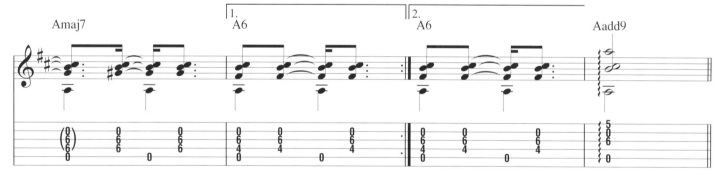

Variation 3

This variation substitutes Pattern 7's dotted eighth notes in the first measure for a typical Brasileirinho-style rhythm.

Recommended Application: Variation on Pattern 7

PATTERN 8

Recommended Application: Use in progressions that include two chords per measure, often at the end of a section, or during a break from the melody. It can also be used within a batida to add an element of surprise.

Track 46

*Not played on repeat.

*Not played on repeat.

MISCELLANEOUS PATTERNS

The following patterns are used much less frequently in the bossa nova repertoire. Further, they are never used as the main batida, but rather are inserted into batidas to add dynamic and variety to the rhythm.

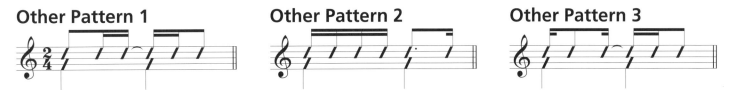

Other Pattern 1   Other Pattern 2   Other Pattern 3

Recommended Application: Use as a variation on Patterns 1, 2, 3, and 4, including different combinations as part of the batida.

These three miscellaneous patterns have been inserted among other patterns and variations in the following practical example. Find them in the arrangement and listen closely to how they add their own particular flavor to the composition.

Track 47

*Not played on repeat.

Chapter 6
COMPLETE SONGS

As in all of styles of popular music, there are no specific rules in bossa nova that tell us exactly which pattern or voicing sounds best for any given situation. It is often the individual style and personality of the musician that colors the performance. The following guidelines should help you keep your playing faithful to the original sound and flavor of this unique musical style.

Here are the first three steps in approaching any bossa nova composition:

- Learn and understand all of the chord voicings presented in Chapter 3, as well as the chord progressions that link them together (vertical and horizontal harmony, respectively).

- Master all of the rhythm patterns taught in Chapter 5.

- Choose one of the rhythm patterns presented in Chapter 5 and use it as the batida.

Let's look at the final point in greater detail. Before you can choose a pattern to be used as the principal batida, you first need to take into consideration the feel, or intention, of the song itself. Most classic bossa nova batidas are built on Patterns 1 and 2, as well as those from samba, which are typically Patterns 3, 4, and 5. Naturally, these batidas are played at different tempos depending upon the song, but in general the first two are played between 60 and 70 bpm, whereas the second three are played from 70 bpm and up.

Once you have defined a tempo and pattern for a section or song, select the characteristic variations to give the song further nuance, be it highlighting a specific section of the arrangement or addiing a fresh rhythmic perspective for the listener.

These variations are key, as experienced Brazilian guitarists tend to play accompaniment as if it were a kind of interaction—a series of calls and responses, so to speak. Small but significant variations can be created through the inclusion or exclusion of tied notes, sixteenth notes, and so on, thus providing the freedom of expression for which bossa nova is so well known.

Let's take a look at an example of this process, using a compound pattern built from Patterns 1 and 2, with a tempo of 60 bpm.

Now, if you substitute two sixteenth notes for the second eighth note of beat 1, you'll have created a dyamic batida. You can then add a muted note at the end of the pattern, and then tack Pattern 4 (which uses the second measure from Pattern 2) onto the end, and you've got a unique rhythm pattern that looks like this:

Here is another example, using Pattern 3 as the batida.

To color this pattern, you can first get rid of the ties that cause the syncopation, and then add two more measures to the pattern with the following modifications:

- Substitute the eighth notes on beat 1 with four sixteenth notes.

- Eliminate the eighth note in the first Brasileirinho.

- Remove the syncopated note between the first and second measures of the pattern.

- Add one sixteenth note at the end of the pattern, tied to the downbeat of the following measure.

As you can see, using the patterns and variations presented in this book, as well as their source rhythm cells (as found in the table on page 25), will enable you to create unique bossa nova rhythm patterns that will not only demonstrate your style and taste but will also enable you to remain faithful to the roots of the bossa nova sound.

Demonstration Songs

To help you apply the concepts you've learned in this book, here are two complete song arrangements. The chord voicings, progressions, and rhythmic patterns used in these songs are based on well-known and highly respected bossa nova compositions, to give you an authentic taste of the style.

Each song has two audio tracks. The first is a complete demo, including the guitar. The second is a play-along backing track, without guitar, thus allowing you to become the guitarist in the ensemble.

SONG 1

SONG 2

Full Band
Track 50

Play-along
Track 51

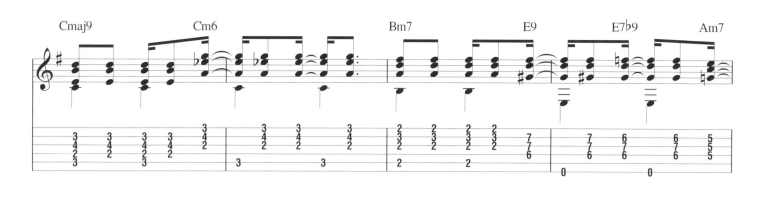

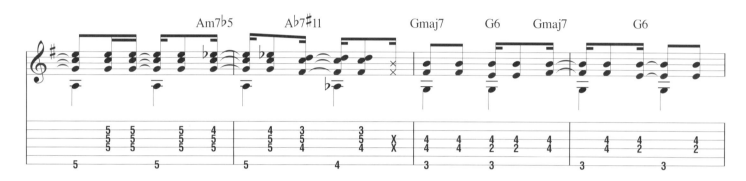

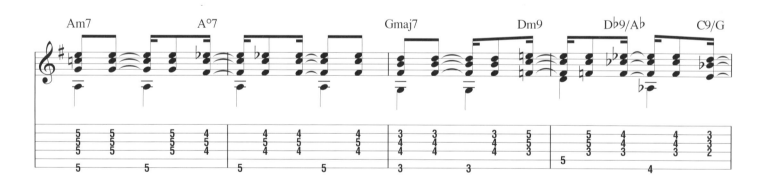

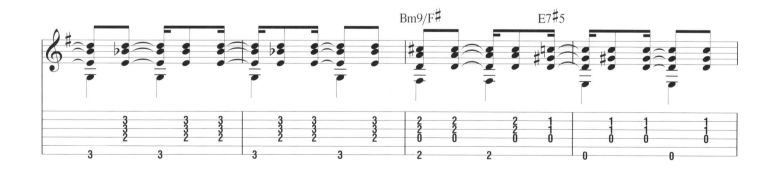

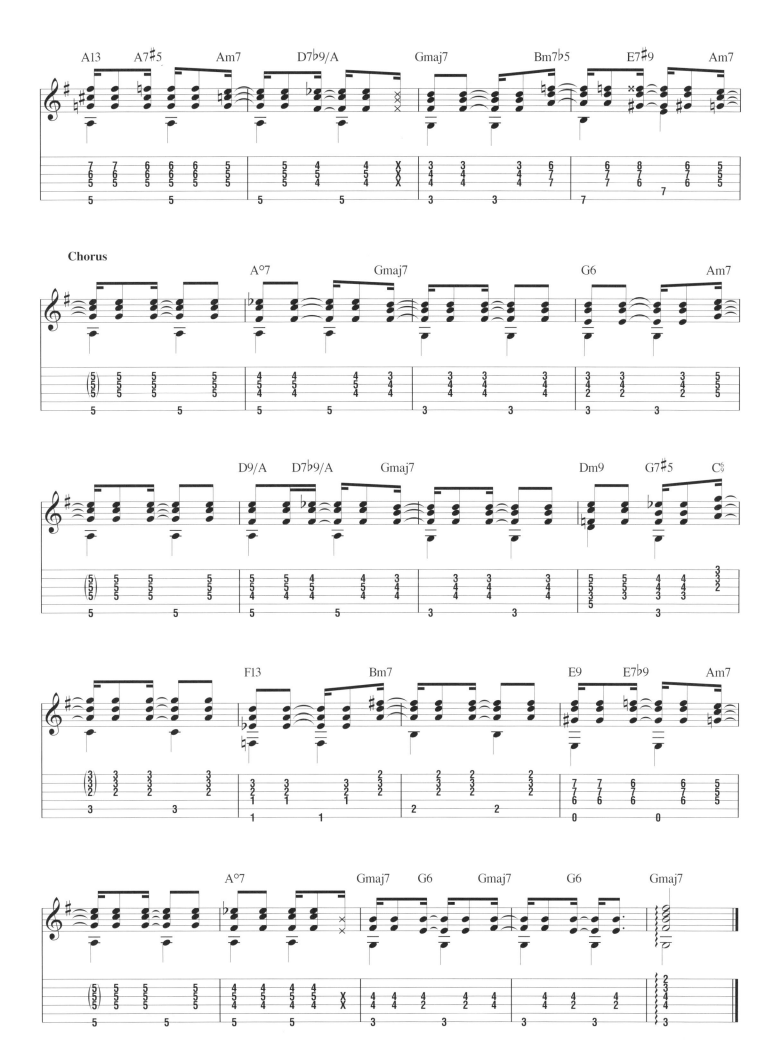

Guitar Notation Legend

Guitar Music can be notated three different ways: on a *musical staff*, in *tablature*, and in *rhythm slashes*.

RHYTHM SLASHES are written above the staff. Strum chords in the rhythm indicated. Use the chord diagrams found at the top of the first page of the transcription for the appropriate chord voicings. Round noteheads indicate single notes.

THE MUSICAL STAFF shows pitches and rhythms and is divided by bar lines into measures. Pitches are named after the first seven letters of the alphabet.

TABLATURE graphically represents the guitar fingerboard. Each horizontal line represents a string, and each number represents a fret.

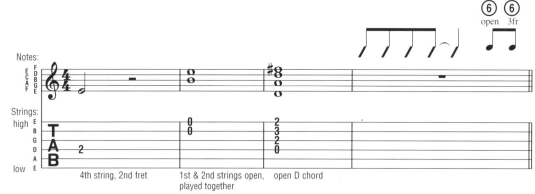

4th string, 2nd fret   1st & 2nd strings open, played together   open D chord

HALF-STEP BEND: Strike the note and bend up 1/2 step.

WHOLE-STEP BEND: Strike the note and bend up one step.

GRACE NOTE BEND: Strike the note and immediately bend up as indicated.

SLIGHT (MICROTONE) BEND: Strike the note and bend up 1/4 step.

BEND AND RELEASE: Strike the note and bend up as indicated, then release back to the original note. Only the first note is struck.

PRE-BEND: Bend the note as indicated, then strike it.

VIBRATO: The string is vibrated by rapidly bending and releasing the note with the fretting hand.

WIDE VIBRATO: The pitch is varied to a greater degree by vibrating with the fretting hand.

HAMMER-ON: Strike the first (lower) note with one finger, then sound the higher note (on the same string) with another finger by fretting it without picking.

PULL-OFF: Place both fingers on the notes to be sounded. Strike the first note and without picking, pull the finger off to sound the second (lower) note.

LEGATO SLIDE: Strike the first note and then slide the same fret-hand finger up or down to the second note. The second note is not struck.

SHIFT SLIDE: Same as legato slide, except the second note is struck.

TRILL: Very rapidly alternate between the notes indicated by continuously hammering on and pulling off.

TAPPING: Hammer ("tap") the fret indicated with the pick-hand index or middle finger and pull off to the note fretted by the fret hand.

NATURAL HARMONIC: Strike the note while the fret-hand lightly touches the string directly over the fret indicated.

PINCH HARMONIC: The note is fretted normally and a harmonic is produced by adding the edge of the thumb or the tip of the index finger of the pick hand to the normal pick attack.

PICK SCRAPE: The edge of the pick is rubbed down (or up) the string, producing a scratchy sound.

MUFFLED STRINGS: A percussive sound is produced by laying the fret hand across the string(s) without depressing, and striking them with the pick hand.

PALM MUTING: The note is partially muted by the pick hand lightly touching the string(s) just before the bridge.

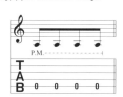

RAKE: Drag the pick across the strings indicated with a single motion.

TREMOLO PICKING: The note is picked as rapidly and continuously as possible.

VIBRATO BAR DIVE AND RETURN: The pitch of the note or chord is dropped a specified number of steps (in rhythm) then returned to the original pitch.

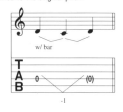

VIBRATO BAR SCOOP: Depress the bar just before striking the note, then quickly release the bar.

VIBRATO BAR DIP: Strike the note and then immediately drop a specified number of steps, then release back to the original pitch.